MW01089927

Galicia Travel Guide

*Sightseeing, Hotel, Restaurant
& Shopping Highlights*

Emily Sutton

If there are any errors or omissions in copyright acknowledgements the publisher will be pleased to insert the appropriate acknowledgement in any subsequent printing of this publication.

Table of Contents

A Coruña, Vigo & Costa do Marisco

Avoid the crowded beaches of the well known costas of Spain and head to the Galician coastline instead for a refreshing and sunny change. In the Costa do Marisco (Shellfish Coast), the Norwegian-style fjords of the Rias Altas hide deserted beaches, shallow lagoons and pretty little villages where freshly caught fish and shellfish are plentiful on local menus.

Try the expensive and interesting "percebes" or goose barnacles. The scourge of a sailor's life, these weird looking crustaceans have been eaten for years by the Galician people and are now regarded as a local designer dish.

The densely wooded areas of Galicia hide a wealth of wildlife and in most places the forests and surrounding countryside are unpolluted. The landscapes of the RiasBaixas make this province one of the most beautiful in Spain and get their name from the five flooded valleys in the area. Visitors to the Galician countryside will be puzzled by the many buildings perched on stilts with a cross on the roof. These "horreos" are not religious shrines as many people would imagine but traditional grain stores. They are very rarely used now for their original purpose but are an important part of Galician history and "horreos" souvenirs are available all over the province.

Culture

The architecture and culture of the Costa do Marisco dates from Roman times and there are many interesting ruins to see in the cities and all around the province. The Roman Wall of Lugo isthe finest example in western Europe of Roman fortification and is a World Heritage Site.

Contained within the boundaries of the Costa Do Marisco is the Costa da Muerte or coast of death. Stretching from Malpica in the north to Fisterra in the south the treacherous rocks have been responsible for many shipwrecks and loss of life. Fishing is a main income in this area and around 90,000 fishermen catch 50% of Spain's fish.

Being Spain there are enough ferias and fiestas to keep even the most dedicated party lover busy. The biggest is in Santiago de Compostela in July and is the festival of St James the Apostle. Celebrations begin with fireworks in Obradoiro Square on the eve of the Day of the Apostle including the burning of the cathedral façade. The following day offerings are made inside the cathedral to St James and then the parade of giant figures takes to the street.

In October every year 200,000 people make the journey to O Grove for the Fiesta de Exaltación de Marisco. Clams, crab, mussels and fish stew are all on the menu so if you are a fish lover why not plan your trip around this time.

For something a little more dangerous why not go to Laza in Ourense for the OsPeliqueiros Carnival in February/March. The OsPeliqueiros run through the streets waving sticks, the sound of the cowbells on their belts adding to the general noise and cacophony. Wearing outrageous costumes and masks they are allowed to lash out at the crowds who must take the punishment and not hit back.

Wine festivals, flower festivals, history festivals, festivals to celebrate Christopher Columbus and even a festival to cut the tails off wild horses. Yes, it's true, in Pontevedra the horse fair "A Rapa das Bestas" has been turned from a yearly chore into a round of partying. Well, it is Spain after all!

Location & Orientation

On the northwest corner of Spain the Costa de Marisco starts close to A Coruña in the north and finishes south of Vigo near the Spanish-Portuguese border. Facing the Atlantic the coast has been battered over thousands of years by high seas and strong winds and the results can be seen in the intriguing rocky coastline.

A Coruña airport serves the northern part of the coast but the flights are mostly domestic and to the Spanish islands with one international flight to Amsterdam on a seasonal basis. Vigo in the southern part is also mostly domestic with one international destination, Paris. The airport at Santiago de Compostela is the biggest in Galicia and there are more international flights to here as well as domestic ones. A route between the city and London-Gatwick is due to open in June 2013.

There are train stations in all the major towns and cities and direct rail connections across the border into Portugal. An AVE (high speed) station is being constructed in Porto to accommodate the trains that will eventually run on the new line from A Coruña, through Vigo and into Portugal. The line is due to be operational by 2016.

Climate & When to Visit

The Galician climate is similar to the climate in the Pacific North West of North America with warm, dry summers and mild winters.

The area does get rainfall throughout the year and this makes sure the verdant green landscapes remain so. The sometimes-heavy rainfall sweeps in from the Atlantic turning to snow on the higher ground in winter. Vigo has slightly warmer summers and milder winters due to the sheltered location while to the north A Coruña has mild weather but more uniform rainfall through the year.

For anyone that wants to visit Spain in the summer months but doesn't want the heat of the more southern areas the Costa do Marisco and Galicia could be the answer. In July and August the average daily temperature is around 18° C with lows of 15°C and highs of 21.5°c. In winter the average is 14°C dropping down to around 9°C.

The summer weather is still warm enough for sunbathing so light clothing is an essential part of your wardrobe but maybe add a light cardigan or jacket for evenings. An advantage of these lower temperatures means that sightseeing and sleeping are more pleasurable without the hot, sticky heat normally associated with Spain. If you are visiting in the winter months bring a raincoat and umbrella. It might not be that cold but it could be very wet.

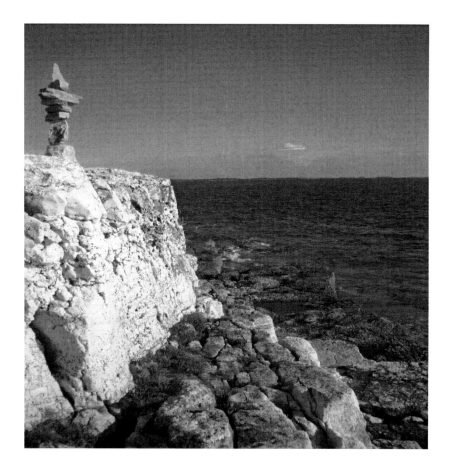

Sightseeing Highlights

Santiago de Compostela

http://www.santiagoturismo.com/

The city of Santiago de Compostela is one end of the
European long distance walking route E3, or the Camino
de Santiago as the Spanish part is better known.

The 6,950km (4,320) path takes 350 days to complete the whole route and goes through France, Belgium, Luxembourg, Germany, the Czech Republic, Poland, Slovakia, Hungary, along the Black Sea coast into Bulgaria to end at Cape Emine. If you don't have year to spare hiking through Europe a visit to Santiago is still a must do. Santiago is a beautiful city full of history and stunning architecture. Some of the places not to miss are:

Plaza de Obradoiro, the largest square of its kind in Galicia. The plaza takes its name from "Obra de Oro" or work of gold and certainly wasn't named for its colour but maybe for the richness of the buildings on all four sides. They are all of incredible historical interest and are:

Santiago Cathedral: A Romanesque structure with Baroque and Gothic additions and one of the most splendid in the country.

The Hospital Real: Founded in 1489 by the Catholic Monarchs, it is now a luxurious parador and is set in four courtyards with a Gothic chapel in the centre dating from 1556.

Palacio de Gelmirez: On the east side is the Archbishop's Palace. A plain looking building which hides the Palacio de Gelmirez, one of the most important secular buildings in Spain. The 30m /100ft long Salòn de Fiestas and Sala des Armas are very popular with tourists as is the second floor medieval kitchen.

Palacio de Rajoy: Designed by a Frenchman, Charles Lemaur, the neo-classical building faces the Cathedral. Today it is used as the town hall and parliament building but has in the past been used as a prison.

In the area round the Plaza de Obradoiro are numerous smaller squares, full of interesting buildings and worth investigating. For walking tours of the city an official guide will take you on a two hour walk where you will get a fascinating glimpse into the history behind the old stone walls of Santiago. The tours are in Spanish and/or English and depart from the tourist office. The old town tour is Tuesday and Saturday at 1pm from June to October and Sunday at 1pm for the rest of the year. Prices are €15 per adult and €5 per child. From the tourist office you can book a guided tour of some of the local workshops and see firsthand some of the ancient trading customs of the town: leather, traditional braiding, silverwork and jet stone.

For shopaholics the choice is endless, the three modern shopping centres where you can find all you need under one roof are Área Central' Shopping Centre, As Cancelas and Compostela Shopping Centre.With easy car parking, cinemas, restaurants and play areas for the little ones sometimes this can be the easiest option. Find the Ensanche area in the town centre where tourists and pilgrims rub shoulders with locals going about their daily business.

There are individual shops as well as international names plus a huge selection of bars, cafeterias and restaurants. The best way is just to wander through the streets stopping off for a drink and tapas as the mood takes you. There are several themed markets for a spot of outdoor browsing and the traffic free Salgueiriños market is the biggest general market for clothes and shoes, bed and table linen. There is also a Hippy market selling handmade local crafts, the Cattle market and an Antiques market.

Santiago is home to three hotel and catering colleges and the gastronomy of the city reflects the association of training and good food. The Santiago Gastronomic Guide is an excellent book to learn about local ingredients and where to go and whatto try. Having a long coastline means there are plenty of fishy delights to try and traditionally the best months for fish are months with an "r" in. Galician style octopus is one of the most popular dishes, simply octopus cooked with cayenne pepper and olive oil and for non-fish lovers there is "caldogallego" (Galician stew) made with potatoes and smoked pig fat among other things.

Look out for the "tarta de Santiago" a traditional dessert made with almonds and topped by a layer of icing sugar bearing the Apostle's cross. For cheese lovers the distinct conical shape of the "queso de tetilla" is easy to find and Santiago has many other locally produced cheeses. Galician wines from theRíasBaixas and Ribeira Sacra regions are delicious as is the most well-known wine of the area, Ribiero. Keep the witches and goblins away by finishing off a meal with a queimada or flamed eau-de-vie. The spell that is chanted while this drink is being made from an herb liqueur and other ingredients will keep you safe.

A Coruña

A Coruña sits on a peninsula at the northwest corner of Spain. Hundreds of years ago it was only a tiny strip of land but the buildup of sand due to sea currents has made it into the size it is today.
It was from this isthmus that the ill-fated Spanish Armada departed from in 1588 only to be wiped out by Sir Francis Drake and the British navy. A Coruña is one of only eight cities in the world to have a nearly exact antipodean opposite, in this case Christchurch in New Zealand.

The major part of the town is built on the rocky promontory with the sea crashing on the rocks all around. The promenade, all 13 kilometres of it, runs through the coves, cliff and beaches and right round the headland. While lovers of aqua sports take up surfing, kayaking and sailing the landlubbers stick to walking, cycling and skating round the smooth path and admiring the views.

The Avenida de la Marina by the port with thousands of galleried windows reflecting the light is a spectacular sight. Originally built as houses for fishermen the extra layer of glass was put into keep the rain and spray from getting into the houses. A Coruña is often referred to as Crystal City and there can be amazing light pattern from the sun and reflected in the glass.

The pedestrianised streets are packed with restaurants, tapas bars and shops mixed in with the medieval buildings and squares. When all the hustle and bustle gets too much take a break and visit the beautiful beaches of Orzan and Riazor in the central part of the city opposite the port.

To experience some of A Coruñas beautiful architecture and history some of the best places to visit in the town are:

The Tower of Hercules: The 55m/180ft lighthouse is the oldest Roman lighthouse in use today and it is a World Heritage Site and National Monument of Spain.

The Santiago Church: Built in the 12th century and the oldest church in A Coruña.

A Coruña Museum of Fine Arts: From contemporary art to Rodin, from sculpture to paintings, there is lot to see in this museum housed in a beautiful old convent.

The Monte de San Pedro Park and panoramic lift: Stunning views from the top of this very unusual spherical glass lift.

Vigo

Vigo is one of the major economic and industrial cities in Galicia with the Port of Vigo being the largest in Europe and one of the busiest for sea traffic. With car manufacturing plants, shipyards and all the associated smaller industries the GDP of Galicia is mostly provided by Vigo. Pescanova, the world's largest fishing company has their home here as do many other famous names in the industry. Fish is exported from here to Portugal, Italy, France and as far afield as Asia.

Nowadays tourism is becoming one of the most booming industries in Vigo. Tourists who want to see more than the port, shipyards and car plants won't be disappointed and the Romanesque ruins a few kilometres from the city centre are a good place to start.

Three of the churches in Vigo are extremely important examples of Romanesque architecture in Galicia and are worth visiting.

After the death of Franco in 1975, the 1980's saw a newly liberated Vigo become home to punk and new wave bands. While many of the bands didn't last long a few of the more notorious ones still call Vigo home. A film based on the memories of the Port of Vigo workers losing their jobs was filmed here with the title Los Lunes al Sol (*Mondays In The Sun*).

Vigo has more to offer than containers and cruise ships; the sparking, glitzy marina is home to one of the most exclusive yachting clubs in Spain, Real Club Náutico de Vigo. The Casco Vello (old town) is welcoming and everywhere there are bars and restaurants full of Galician people enjoying life. There is a distinct lack of trashy souvenir shops despite the thousands of people that pour into the town off the cruise ships. The locals go about their business and if you want to experience a proper Galician town Vigo will be hard to beat.

For shopping try Casco Vello and La Piedra Market: Higgledy-piggledy streets with tiny shops and the market where you can buy homemade products like cakes, bread and cheese. Príncipe and Urzaiz streets are surrounded by beautiful architecture and there are some of the most fashionable boutiques and famous names in this more modern commercial area.

For a walk in the fresh head for the Celtic Castro ruins. Sandwiched between the leisure parks and nearby forest the Monte de Castro mount has the best views of the city. When the cobwebs have blown away find the Cathedral of Santa Maria which is great for a history lesson and was built between 1816 and 1836 as a replacement for the former Gothic church.

San Carlos Garden

Paseo del Parrote
15001 A Coruña

Perched high above the town there are some excellent views of the port and San Anton Castle below. The fortress in the park was built in 1843 and is in the old San Carlos bastion. John Moore, an English general who died in battle was laid to rest here and his tomb and bronze bust are both very interesting. These beautiful and romantic gardens are often used for wedding photography.

Monte de San Pedro Park

A Coruña

The huge expanse of land that has been made into a park for everyone to enjoy used to belong to the Spanish military, the lookout turrets, barracks and underground passageways have been restored and can be explored to give an insight into the life of a soldier. Located high up on the cliffs the soldiers would have an excellent view of any marauding ships trying to enter into the city and the huge cannons still in situ show how seriously the defence of this area was taken. For some light amusement there is a maze with Italian trees and a children's play area.

The park has two distinct attractions; the Cúpula Atlántica, a dome shaped building with 360ª views and the Ascensor (lift) de San Pedro. This spherical glass lift will take you up the cliff side from the car park to the top of the park in just four minutes. A return ticket costs €3. Entry to the park is free and the gates are open from 11am to 8pm in winter and 11am to 10pm in summer.

Galicia Marine Museum

160 Avenida Atlántida
36208 Vigo
+34 986 247 750
http://museodomar.xunta.es

The museum is in the Punta de Muiño area of Vigo and the buildings that make up the complex are right on the edge of the Atlantic Ocean. The museum is dedicated to the heritage of the sea and there is a lighthouse with spectacular views and an aquarium where the Rias of the Galician system are explained. You can learn about the fishing and preservation methods, old and new, shell fishing and the impact of new technology on the vessels used. The museum is open morning and evening with a break for siesta and the hours vary according to the time of year. The entry fee is €3 for adults and younger children are free.

Vigo Municipal Museum

Parque de Castrelos s/n
36213, Vigo
+34 986 295 070
www.museo.devigo.org

Housed in one of Vigo's most beautiful buildings the museum has a fascinating collection of archaeological remains that have be found in the city during excavations and a display of Galician paintings.

The palace housing the museum was built in the 1670's and restoration work was carried out late 19th and early 29th century. Located in Castrelos Park the gardens have fountains and pools and are designed in a French style. The admission is free and the opening times vary from all day to half days and days with siestas. It would be better to check the website or call before visiting.

Vigo Zoo

Plaza de los Leones,
36316, Madroa - Teis,
Vigo
+34 986 267 783
www.vigozoo.com

Vigo Zoo has a wide diversity of trees and plants that blend in well with the surrounding area and covers an area of 55,676 m2. There are around 45 types of birds, 24 mammals, 30 reptiles as well as insects, spiders and butterflies in the enclosures which have been designed with the natural habitat of the animals taken into careful consideration. The Zoo is open all year around but is closed on Mondays except on Bank Holidays, for adults the entrance fee is €5 but there are a wide variety of discounts available.

Cies Island & Nature Reserve

Vigo

The Cies Islands are a cluster of uninhabited islands that act as a barrier protecting the Rias from violent winds and make a natural safe harbour. There are three main islands; Monte Faro, San Martino and Monteaguada along with the smaller islets of Vinos, O Ruzo, Agoeira and Carabelos. There are many types of flora and fauna living safely on the islands as they were declared a natural park in 1980 and in 2002 became part of the Atlantic Isles Nature Reserve.

The amazing Cíes Islands have the best beach in the world according to a report by The Guardian newspaper in 2007 but if lazing on the white sand looking at the clear, sparkling water gets too boring there are well-defined walking paths and plenty of bird watching. Early evidence shows that the islands were first occupied in the Iron Age and later by the Romans, but constant invasions from the Normans and pirates didn't make for a peaceful existence and in the 1700's the islands were abandoned. A lighthouse was built here in the 19th century but today the only occupants are the game wardens.

There is a small campsite with all the necessary facilities, a shop and a couple of restaurants. Everything, including the menus is in Spanish only so a phrase book might be handy if you are not familiar with the language.

The only access to cover the 14km between Vigo and the largest of the islands is by a 45 minute ferry ride from Vigo, Baiona or Cangas. The ferries run from Easter to September and tickets are strictly limited so booking is advisable. The one vehicle on the island belongs to the park ranger so walking is the only way to get to those deserted coves and beautiful beaches.

Naval Museum and Exponav

Edificio Herrerías
Cantón Molins
15403, Ferrol
+34 981 336 000
www.exponav.org

The museum has information on all the ships built in the area from 1751 to 1984 along with permanent exhibitions of models, flags, weapons, diving suits and a whole host of other sea related items. Exponav is an exhibition of the history of shipbuilding from the Middle Ages to the present day. Opening times are Tuesday to Friday 9.30am to 1.30pm and weekends and holidays from 10.30am to 1.30pm.

Ferrol has two claims to fame; in the 17th century it was the biggest military arsenal in Europe and in 1892 it was the birthplace of General Francisco Franco. Ferrol town centre takes its inspiration from Lisbon in Portugal and is basically a rectangle with two squares on either side and six parallel streets that are home to the best galleries, shops, bars and restaurants.

Ferrol is very much a Spanish working town but there are some beautiful beaches north of the town and the Castillo de San Felipe is worth visiting.

Parque Natural Fragas do Eume

Oficina del Parque Natural de Fragas do Eume
Lugar de Esteiro 23, 15600
+34 981495580
www.viveaonatural.xunta.es/

The park covers an area of some 9,000 square hectares and is covered with a wide variety of trees, from cork trees growing on the sunny south side to lichens and moss clinging onto the damp north facing rocks. The natural park is full of lush vegetation with some wonderful walks through the fairy tale woods dappled with shade from the canopy of oak trees. Close to the Pontedeume side of the park is an old monastery and there is a free bus service in high season if you don't wish to walk. After travelling hundreds of kilometres the river Eume wriggles through the oaks in the forest before spilling out into an estuary and the sea.

In the town of Pontedeume there is a visitor centre at the park entrance although there are four other points of entry around the perimeter allowing access to the different areas. You can get details of the park at the visitor centre and information about the set walking trails of different levels. The park was subject to fire in March 2012 and some of the more important areas were affected but not the monastery or the homes of the 500 people who live in the park.

Fervenza do Toxa

Located between Silleda and Merza
Pontevedra

For hiking, waterfalls and nature take a trip to the
Fervenza La Toja just north of Silleda, Pontevedra. The
Tojariver pours over the rocks from a height of 60 metres
creating a spectacular waterfall in the midst of a beautiful
green landscape. Picnic benches and seats directly
opposite the tumbling waters offer a welcome place to
rest after a walk through the woods. If you visit in the
summer months take a swimming costume and towels as
there are tranquil pools where you can stop for a cooling
dip.

Look out for fauna that is mostly associated with rivers.
Badgers, otters and weasels can often be seen along with
many trout splashing about in the clear waters while
peregrine falcons fly overhead.

Illa de Arousa

Pontevedra
http://www.ailladearousa.com

Connected to the mainland by a two-kilometre bridge is
the Illa de Arousa. In the census 2011 around 5,000 people
lived on the tiny seven square kilometre island which is
the only island municipality in Galicia.

Measuring about four km from one end to the other there are several neighbourhoods and one church. The lighthouse at Cabalo Point stands tall on the granite rocks keeping guard over the rocks and beaches scattered along the coastline. The narrowest point of the island is a mere 200 metres wide and passing through the houses on this tiny strip makes you wonder about high tide.

The far side of the island is more open and it is worth the walk to see the weirdly shaped rocks and keep a look out for the one shaped like a Gremlin. If you decide to walk to take advantage of the views from the lighthouse then end your trip at the bar where you can enjoy a refreshing drink. In the main part of the town the harbor is home to hundreds of little fishing boats gently bobbing up and down at anchor in the bays and moored up at the many jetties.

Needless to say there are of course bars and restaurants for you enjoy freshly caught fish, prepared Galician style of course.

Aquapark de Cerceda

Polígono do Acevedo s/n
15185 Cerceda - A Coruña
+ 34 981 685 036
http://www.aquapark.cerceda.org

Aquapark de Cerceda is the only park of its kind in Galicia and while it might not be the biggest waterpark in the world there is more than enough to keep the family amused for a day out.

There are plenty of pools of all shapes and sizes along with a wave pool, roller coaster ride, aquatubo, kamikaze and slides of varying lengths. There is a playpark for the little ones, a caféteria and plenty of space to sunbathe with lockers, sunbeds and umbrellas for hire. The park is open for the summer months from mid-June to mid-September from 10 noon to 8pm. Adult prices are €7 weekdays and €8 at the weekends, while children pay €5 weekdays and €6 at the weekends.

Recommendations for the Budget Traveller

Places To Stay

La Pensión Palacio

Plaza de Galicia, Nº2, 4ºD
15004
La Coruña
+34 981 122 338

La Pensión de Palacio has been open for more than 50 years and is owned and run by Manolo and Flora.

Ideally located in the beautiful Plaza de Galicia the Pensión welcomes guests for both long and short stays, as well as students. There is a restaurant, a laundry service plus parking and garage spaces available. If you want to bring your pet with you, he or she will be more than welcome.

Everything you could need is within 100 metres of your accommodation including bars, shops, restaurants, supermarkets and chemists. Another couple of hundred metres or so further and you will find some of the most attractive and important parks in La Coruña. Room prices are reasonable at €19 for a single, €28 for a double and €38 for a triple room. All the rooms have washbasins but the other facilities are shared.

Hostal Riá de Vigo

Rúa de Cervantes, 14
36201, Vigo
+34 986 437 240
www.hostalriadevigo.com

The hostal is in the centre of Vigo and with only ten rooms you will be treated like one of the family during your stay. The sea is only a few steps away and in the Old Town nearby you will find plenty of artisan craft shops. There is plenty going on in the surrounding area with museums, theatres, cultural centres and of course there are lots of restaurants where you can try some delicious fish dishes or typical Galician cuisine.

There are single, double and triple bedded rooms to choose from and all the rooms have private bathrooms, heating, television and Wifi. There are rooms available for smokers and pets are accepted. Single rooms cost €20, double €25 / €30 and triple €45 and €55.

Pensión Badalada

Rúa Xelmírez 30, 15704
Santiago de Compostela
+34 981 572 618
www.badalada.es

Pensión Badalada is on a slight incline in the maze of streets surrounding the Cathedral and you can wake to the sound of the bells in the morning. The pension opened in 2008 and is in an antique house that has been tastefully restored with local stone and wood to create an intimate atmosphere.

The rooms are beautifully decorated and have private bathrooms. The communal areas are warm and welcoming and the staff are very friendly and will do their utmost to help you. For anyone wanting to walk the Camino de Santiago there is a luggage storage room to leave your belongings in for a small fee. Room prices are from €35 for a single room and €49 for a double.

Hostal Colón Riviera

Rúa Cristóbal Colón nº 29
Santa Eugenia de Riviera
+ 34 981 870 415
www.hostalcolonriveira.com/

This two star hostel is a stone's throw from the seafront and offers comfortable accommodation in a family run business that opened in 1988. A few metres away is the local church and all the historical and cultural sights that the town has to offer.

There is a fully stocked bar and breakfast is available in the wood panelled restaurant. The 22 rooms have private bathrooms, television, central heating, hairdryers and free Wifi. Cots and irons are available on request free of charge. Individual rooms are priced from €24 and double rooms from €30.

Hostal J.B.

Rúa Playa, 3
Malpica De Bergantiños
15113 La Coruña
Teléfono: 981 721 906
www.hostaljb.es

Hostal J.B. is 52km from the capital of A Coruña and is set in a super location. The little town has the harbor on one side and a beautiful curving sandy beach on the other.

The hostel is situated on the seafront and is ideal for a tranquil stay on this wonderful part of Spain. The rooms all have private bathroom, television and heating. There is a lift and free Wifi. Some of the rooms have terraces with a sea view. A double room is priced from €30 and a single room from €20.

Places To Eat & Drink

Restaurante Boga

Concepcion Arenal 7,
36201Vigo,
+34 886 125 854

A small café-bar that is a great place for a drink or a light meal. In the warmer months the tables outside are ideal to sit and watch the locals going about their business. The beer is well priced and comes with free tapas. There is a good selection of wines to go with the menu of seafood, tapas and typical Spanish dishes. Expect to pay somewhere between €11to €26 for a meal.

O Piorno

Rua Caldeira, 24,
Santiago de Compostela,
+34 881 259 002
www.opiorno.com

The old building that houses O Piorno used to be a haberdashery and care has been taken to try and keep some of the atmosphere of years gone by. The restaurant is bright and modern but still retains a certain charm and the portions are large and the staff friendly and attentive. One of the house specialties is octopus weighing around 1.5kg cooked with olive oil, sweet and spicy pepper. The prices range from €13 to €26.

Restaurante O Elefante

Azibechería, 5 (Zona Vella)
15704, Santiago de Compostela
+34 902 091 466 ext. 8776

O Elefante is a vegetarian restaurant with a menu full of surprises with not just well known dishes but homemade creations that include their own brand of veggie nut burger. They also serve a wonderful range of healthy drinks and milk shakes and have homemade vegetarian desserts. Only a few steps from the Cathedral at night the restaurant becomes alive with the addition of cocktails. There is a terrace, access for disabled guests and pets are welcome outside.

Open Monday, Wednesday and Sunday from 9am to 1.30am, Thursday, Friday and Saturday from 9am to 3.30am. Closed Tuesdays. To find the restaurant head for Plaza de Cervantes, look for the Azibecheria Museum and O Elefante is in one of the narrow streets close by.

Restaurante-Raxería El Rubio

Hersa, 8
Culleredo,
15670, A Coruña
+34 657 551 882

Raxeria El Rubio is located in a pedestrian street and serves traditional Gallegan cooking. They serve tapas, meals and a special menú El Rubio. Their specialties are Raxa and Zorza which are pork loin dishes cooked in two different ways. For fish lovers try the bacalao a la nata (cod in cream) or the unmistakable flavours of freshly cooked trout. For families there is a children's menu as well as a garden area with play equipment. There is disabled access and free Wifi. El Rubio is open every day apart from Tuesday from 10am to close. The daily menu is good value at less than €15 and there is an á la carte menu if you prefer to choose something different.

Nueva Tapería La Abuela

San Lorenzo, 22
Baiona, 36300
Pontevedra
+34 902 091 466 ext.8819

The old medieval town of Baiona has much to offer and situated a few streets from the harbour and the Convento de Dominicas is Tapería La Abuela. More of a snack bar than a restaurant they offer pizzas, burgers, snack and sandwiches and a menu of the day. On Mondays there is a special offer of a drink and tapas for only €1, at other times the prices are still great and most items including the daily menu are less than €15. Open seven days a week from 9am to 2am.

Places To Shop

Mercado de Abastos de Santiago

Rúa das Ameas,
15704 Santiago de Compostela
34 981 58 34 38
http://www.mercadodeabastosdesantiago.com/

The original building that housed the market was demolished in 1937 making room for the current one that opened in 1941.

The high curved ceiling of the fresh food market has many arched windows flooding the hustle and bustle with light. The old Spanish señoras dressed in black crowd round the stalls and select the best produce, shouting at the stall owners for attention.

There are all types of goods available from fruit to fowl and fish, bakeries, butchers and bookshops, flowers and frozen food, clothes and key cutting.

An innovative market, you can take your fresh produce to the bar outside and for a few euros have it cooked while you wait. Fresh milk is available from a vending machine, bring your own bottles or buy on site. The market is open from Monday to Saturday from 7am to 3pm.

C.C. Marineda City

Carretera de Baños de Arteixo, N 43
15008, A Coruña
+34 881 888 888
www.marinedacity.es

This is a mega-shopping centre with something for all the family. There is a cinema, a bowling alley, a brilliant kids zone and a karting track plus an arcade for the over 18's. The children are cared for by the qualified staff while parents wander round the shops or have a peaceful lunch on the restaurant floor lined with palm trees under the glass roof.

There is a huge variety of shops spread over the three floors with fashion, shoes, beauty, furniture, sports goods, electrical and much more from internationally known shops. There are also shops selling locally produced crafts and crafts from Galicia and northeast Spain. The shopping centre is open Monday to Saturday from 10am to 10 pm and the restaurants and leisure activities are open from Sunday to Thursday from 12 noon until midnight and Fridays, Saturdays and fiesta days from 12 noon to 1am. The arcade is open from 12 noon until 11pm.

Kailua Kayak (Windsurfing & Kitesurfing)

Ruá Escultor Gregorio Fernández, 14
36204 Vigo
+ 34 986 227 533
www.kailuakayak.es

For water sports enthusiasts there cannot be a better place to go. The 300m2 shop has everything you could need and more for spending thrilling days both on and in the water. Whether you are looking for a small item to make your kit complete or are a beginner wanting advice and all the necessary equipment, the staff at Kailua Kayak are friendly, knowledgeable and attentive. They hold open days where equipment can be tried out to see if you are choosing the right sport and the shop even has its own Kailua windsurf team. There is a huge selection of kayaks, canoes, boards and sails and clothing, wetsuits, helmets as well, plus some really good discounts on secondhand equipment.

Fish Auctions

Any of the fishing harbours will have fish auctions and it a brilliant way to see how the fishermen sell their catch and how the restaurants and shops haggle for the best price. The "nasas" (fishing baskets) are set the previous day and when the fishing boats return to harbour the fish is auctioned off, usually in the afternoon. Lobsters and crabs are always found at the afternoon auctions as are clams, goose barnacles and cockles which depend on the tidal conditions. May, June, July and August are classed as the "closed" season for shellfish so if you are after crabs and clams perhaps time your visit for the winter months.

If you don't fancy braving the quayside try the busy fish markets of San Augustin and Santa Lucia in A Coruña, or the Municipal Market in Pontevedra and for something smaller the local market at Bueu, close to Vigo. Nearly every coastal town will have a fish market and once you have seen the shiny bodies of the freshly caught fish and caught the tang of the sea you will be off to the nearest restaurant to try some of these wonderful delights.

Lacteos Anzuxao

Madriñan, 2
36512 Lalin
Pontevedra
+34 986 794 135
www.lacteosanzuxao.com

In the Deza region is the Pazo de Anzuxao, a fantastic example of local architecture which dates back to 1713 and has been beautifully preserved. For more than forty years the dairy farm here has produced cheeses using traditional Galician methods but before you enjoy the cheeses go for a wander in the peaceful gardens. A team of about a dozen people work at the dairy and produce the famous cone-shaped "tetilla" under their own name of Arzúa-Ulloa, as well as curd cheese, hard, cured cheese and low fat cheeses with semi-skimmed milk. The various processes can be seen and samples tasted with full sized versions available to purchase.

Made in United States
North Haven, CT
15 March 2022

17146003R00024